# BROTHER SALVAGE

2005 AGNES LYNCH STARRETT PRIZE

Pitt Poetry Series

Ed Ochester, Editor

# BROTHER SALVAGE

*poems*

Rick Hilles

UNIVERSITY OF PITTSBURGH PRESS

Published by the University of Pittsburgh Press, Pittsburgh, PA 15260
Copyright © 2006, Rick Hilles
All rights reserved
Manufactured in the United States of America
Printed on acid-free paper
10 9 8 7 6 5 4 3 2 1


ISBN 0-8229-5935-6

For my brother

    and mother

    my father

    and sister.

And for our brothers and mothers

    our fathers and sisters.


And for Ted.

# Contents

## III

## IV

I

# Antique Shop Window, Kraków

What if they could speak?: the pawn shop menorahs
      and samovars, the cherubs torn from

their heavens, suspended here in limbo, hanging
      by five black strings thickened in dust,

their gold wings flaking so close to earth; the jewel-
      shaped chandeliers unmoored from ceilings;

the salty waves in stasis on the black marble maiden
      naked to the waist but for the black curtain

blown impossibly into place, held there by a constant
      wind no one else can feel as she remains

in darkness, deprived of her own shadow. What of
      the desk hands pressed against? The chair's

own squat suspicions? The serving sets and hand-
      sewn linens, the almost hallucinatory art

deco patterns on teacups and saucers, and elaborate
      dinner plates? The cracked handblown glass,

and not its maker, held in late afternoon sunlight?

The velvet curtain was already falling, the twentieth
century losing its last gray hairs, when the man
brought back from death safely reentered
the war-ravaged city of his birth; the long shadows
flooded him, filling him with sparrows and broken glass.
He unwrapped himself to bandages of lilac cloud,
the ancient dirt road of river still there and shimmering.
The street-cleaners sprayed the sidewalk, and vendors
steadied their fresh flowers, and fruits, and meats;
one elderly woman's hands like gloves the color
of crushed raspberries held out a fat peach,
the best the season had to offer, or so it seemed—
it was all that he'd longed to touch again and taste
and see and would, he knew, soon mourn,
when he turned his back again on the great river,
the sun warm on his shoulders as he pushed through
the revolving glass doors to the library, imperceptibly
passing the distracted guards to one unlit corridor
where among the higher shelves he brushed off
the dusty volumes with an ecstasy that held him
wide awake in the nightmare—more than anything
now he needed to fill in the years of his exile,
his appetite transforming his native tongue
to a new fluency—the readiness and dexterity
in him surpassed, nearly complete. He raced
through a language transcribed from fire
when on the next page framed in the window
by four sudden prison bar shadows, he saw
the photos—bleary, colorless, but images he knew
and recognized—the Warsaw ghetto's first days:
a crowd of children's faces, some smiling and full.
Electric cable car #61 wearing the Star of David
blurring beside a hand-drawn rickshaw; and after

the typhus, a headshot of the boy smuggler
who hid food in his knickers, lying in a black
pool of blood; a starving woman trying to hold
her grief—and a newborn infant, already dead;
the woman lost consciousness soon afterward.
They were the photographs Tadzik had taken
half a century ago—in the first months
of his own captivity after he smuggled into
the ghetto his birthday present: a loaded
Leica camera with two rolls of film. Now
his left hand moved over the faces, the way
he tended them when they were still alive,
and he scanned the wreckage of a shelled-out
hospital for anything that might hold back
death, a spoon or handkerchief to improvise
a splint; overlooked laudanum for pain.
The sudden fusion of purpose and frenzy
a kind of maddening ecstasy
that held him wide awake in the nightmare.
So that even as he stood holding the faces
of the ghetto dead, the buried lives returned,
resurfacing like water startled from the Carpathians.
The foreheads, still wet and feverish, pressed
back against his fingertips; and late Autumn
rattled the windowpanes.—And he remembered
another runner: a man, like him, in the resistance.
But one with access to the outside world, a man
he somehow met and did not meet on a park bench.
Below a fruitless tree—along the ghetto wall
(a suit!) ashing a smoke said, *Amchu?*—"Friend?"
and Tadzik nodded, lowering his brim, the man
calmly sat and pocketed the shriveled bag of film.
And then, not looking up, the man rose slowly
(slowly!) and walked away. And that was that.
(Then fifty years.) The nightmare was exposed.
And the runner had made it, if only once,
back to the world of fruit and light.

# Brother Salvage: a *genizah*

## *I. Scene from a Failed Documentary*

Slow as the sepia swirls of chocolate
on the bottom of a plate can be smeared
by fork then finger into a mouth, he drops

a dollop of cherry compote into your mug
of steaming hot black tea and stirs, the red
Cyclops' eye of a rented camcorder blinking:

Out of film. It's midnight, and six hours
have passed since the retired physician opened
his door to you. The last time, twenty years ago,

he appeared in a white frock, stethoscope,
black hair—now silver-gray yet thick, pomaded,
and raked back, a high widow's peak.

His voice wavers like a squeaky piano lid.
Imagine the pause before an aria. You think of
the time he pushed his sleeves up past the elbow

to give you an allergy shot, and you first saw
the green number on his forearm and asked
him what it was, and he told you what it was

directly: a prisoner tattoo from Auschwitz-
Birkenau. A quick chill shook through your spine.
And rattles still. You begin snaking a black patch

cord around your forearm in figure eights, mortified
for keeping the man up so late, when he says:
"Won't you please take your seat? I've one more

thing to tell you, something strange." *Strange?*
But there is something in the old man's voice
—a cooling salve, that spreads across your dread.

## II. The Finding of the Book

[An unfamiliar postmark/address—a physician.
Upstate N.Y.—27 October 1978]: *Pardon me*
*for writing out of the blue like this but recently*
*I was attending a dinner party to celebrate*
*a friend's new medical practice and as our host*
*topped off glasses and brought in salads*
*(I don't know about you, but since the war*
*I gag on greens of any kind—too harsh*

*a reminder of the weeds we fought*
*over in the camps to keep from starving)*
*I excused myself from the long table of*
*physicians and ambled up the narrow*
*dimly-lit stairs, my hands moving blindly*
*across the cold gooseflesh of a stucco wall*
*when I struck a switch and my eyes opened*
*on a small museum: Wall-to-wall books.*

*My host's library. On the top shelf I saw*
*a threadbare volume crumbling under glass.*
*Soon I was standing in shadow, turning*
*the fragile pages, awakening to its secret*
*knowledge, my desire and the words blurring.*
*Then I heard a noise at the doorway:*
*the oddly pear-shaped silhouette of my host*
*there his voice saying, "What are you doing?"*

*I held out the book and upon seeing it*
*my friend became enraged. He demanded*
*I return the brittle pages to their glass case*

*at once. (I have since learned that this book,*
*your book, was written the same year as*
*Primo Levi's* Survival at Auschwitz *[1946]*
*though your work remains untranslated.)*
*Next morning I called to apologize, only*

*to learn that my friend would be in Utica*
*all day and returning late. Thinking first*
*only of apology, then I saw a kind of door*
*opening and so, somewhat impulsively,*
*I pressed. I told my friend's wife, Helen,*
*of your book, my interest in it, and asked*
*to borrow it that afternoon. I could not*
*stop myself from asking, and she agreed.*

*Late afternoon, my copy made, the book*
*slid in the mail-slot, and the door opened;*
*Helen invited me in—ostensibly to explain*
*her husband's rage. "Like you and me," she said,*
*"he lost everyone in the Holocaust. Everyone!*
*After the war he moved to America, but when*
*he could, returned to Poland. He had to learn*
*what happened to his family—he took out*

*ads for radio, newspaper, TV. Eventually*
*he learned. Most of his people died at*
*Dachau, Treblinka. He learned their fates.*
*All but that of his favorite brother, Israel.*
*His story eluded him. He gave himself*
*another year. Then—discouraged, broke—*
*he resigned himself to traveling by boat*
*back to the States, when in a Warsaw*

*bookstore, he found his copy of this book."*
*Your book!—and with your blessing,*
*one I would very much like to translate.*

From *The Book of Tadzik* (Foreword):
[April, '45]: "When I was liberated by the Allies
—my life was saved. But I was too numb, too sick,
too frail to comprehend. I had no memory of the days
and weeks and months that passed. Only later

when I regained my full weight was I told
that I'd been counted among the living dead.
The fog enveloping me gradually receded and
I began to dwell more fully among the living.
Six months later, my weight nearly doubled,
my wife and I are planning our future when
something—a terrible, invasive power—descends.
As if these dark smothering wings have lifted me

back to the barren, muddy fields at Birkenau,
I'm led to a cramped room whose bare light
blinds me. I hear the heavy movement of metal
doors, the hot screech of iron bolting closed.
The meager bulb inside this vast, cavernous space
sputters out, and a voice inside the darkness yells:
'Gas!' . . . The burning smell tunnels a labyrinth
in me, and I know I am about to die. . . . Nightly

this vision would return, robbing me of strength
—it fed on my sanity. Soon I began to fear
sleep and would read anything to stay awake.
(Novels, history, medical textbooks. Even poetry!)
Anything. But to no avail! . . . Then one night after
the apparition left me particularly bereft I opened
the light and found a notebook. Pen & ink.
Each night I would spend like this, as if possessed.

The nightmares would come to devour me and
I would stab back at them with pen, pushing
them farther into the shadows. In six months

the nightmares stopped, and I had written a book,
*Seven Hells.* I paid another survivor in the DP
Camp in Stuttgart a cigarette a page to type it up.
An edition of several hundred was printed.
And sold on a card table outside the barbed gates.

Would you believe—it sold out in a week?"
[Smalltown, Ohio: Autumn, 2004] ". . . Somehow
the Polish man in America, the one throwing
the party, found my book and read it. I don't
remember where, or what page, but I mention
his brother many, many times. . . . We met
at Birkenau and rode in the same cattle car
from Birkenau to Sachsenhausen. And later

from Sachsenhausen to Dachau. There was
no other record of the man's brother. Anywhere.
No word in any of the main camp registries.
(RH: I checked; the man's brother's surname
at Dachau was misspelled.) . . . And here I was
writing quite a bit about the man's brother,
my friend, and the man recognized his brother
in my descriptions. That was how he learned

the story of his favorite brother, Israel."

*III. The Book of the Brother*

I. SACHSENHAUSEN (P. 275)

"One night EDWIN breaks down. He moves
his hands resignedly. 'How long can we hold on,
TADZIK?' All day we're kept outside. At night,
we are kept outside. A broad-shouldered figure

in the distance approaches. A voice melodious
and deep: *Why complain, colleague? They didn't
bring us here for a vacation. Be satisfied we do not have
to work.* 'Colleague'—the word and his ease

with it bespeaks intelligence. I move closer
to the man dressed in shadows. Can it be?
My father's Warsaw colleague, also a surgeon;
first name, ISRAEL. I have not completely

recovered from my surprise when something,
a deafening blow, levels me. I awaken and feel
my eardrums have burst. Voices—distant, metallic—
the whispering of shrapnel, the stutter of aeroplanes."

## II. Sachsenhausen (p. 285)

"I had gotten used to EDWIN. He was the only
human I let get close. Someone taps my shoulder.
It is ISRAEL: *Don't let that upset you, TADZIK.*

*Remember we do not know who is better off.* It becomes
colder; I look in envy at my reflection in the windowpane:
a dining area where *Haflinge* like us drink coffee

and warm themselves around a stove. ISRAEL
finds a wooden box, places it against a barrack wall,
inviting me to sit. ISRAEL: *At least here we are protected*

*from the colder drafts.* Voices disperse. The sound
of dishes. There are whole weeks when life
is little more than the quandary of being a man

dressed in flames who must keep running to put
himself out. Our overcoats are lined with frozen
lice. *Yes, friend,* says ISRAEL: *This is how it is*

*when you come to some people as a guest. I just hope*
*that when we have our camp, we shall be better hosts.*
Instead of goodnight, he says: *Be patient.*

∼

Despite their warnings and orders that provisions
are to last two days, not a person in our freight car

out of fifty has one crumb left. Only ISRAEL
has bread for the bleak hour. Now temptation

is too great. He breaks off a piece for himself.
Then one for me. I feel the heat spreading

throughout my limbs. *Long live calories* he says.
We pass Nuremberg at noon and are most pleased

to see the wreckage. As we have learned elsewhere
we do not show the full extent of our happiness."

III. Dachau XI: Bauunternehmung L. Moll (p. 296)

"*It's UNBELIEVABLE!* . . . ISRAEL smolders.
*They have NO food, NO light, NO straw.*

*NO BLANKETS. But they have A GONG!*
*Why in the HELL do they have THAT?*"

## IV. Dachau XI: Bauunternehmung L. Moll (p. 303)

"I spit on one hand, grab a pickaxe, as groups
of *Haflinge* push tall carts loaded with stones.
Others carry bricks and the masonry mix.

Unfinished barrack roofs are covered
with layers of earth. Everything is done
to the astonishing accompaniment of curses

and heavy blows. 'We're in luck,' says MAKS,
'If we complete our task in time, we have been
promised soup.' Our shovels are like lead;

the soil, frozen. We make at the earthy ice
with shovels and bare hands. But this thought
of soup restores us. The gong is sounded

and we continue at our labor. The *Raportfuhrer*
shakes his head in disbelief. Pickaxe strike!
Shovels burrow through! Heaps of soil

grow higher—the dark holes deepening!
By evening, almost done, we remove the last
tree stump. The last axe blow resounds!

Then that ridiculous gong! The workday
done, we wring the moisture from our shirts.
The *Raportfuhrer:* 'Why are you still here?'

he asks, arriving with several armed SS.
'Didn't you hear the gong?' And ISRAEL,
who has the best German among us, reminds

him of his promise. He is sorry. He received
word that the potatoes are in another camp.
But we can fill the hole anyway. As for soup,

he says to the SS: 'Jews are good workers!
Promise them soup and they will complete
even the most difficult tasks, surpassing even

well-fed laborers!' Then to us: 'If you can
do a job like that, you don't need soup! *Raus!*'
. . . We stand there like statues. Our legs refuse

movement. The *Raportfuhrer* peels back a branch
from a tree. The SS remove their belts. Not
one among us runs off or cries under the rain

of heavy blows. Slowly, we collect our tools.
Later that night ISRAEL says: *Remember:*
*Even in our silence, friend, they know*

*the full magnificence of our distaste*."

V. Dachau XI: Bauunternehmung L. Moll (p. 308)

"On the horizon, a dense stand of trees.
Our dream: to reach its protection, away
from winter gun blasts. ISRAEL appears
shrunken and stooped—no longer the man he was;
and MAKS, whose overcoat is too short, avoids
the wind by standing between ISRAEL and me

as ISRAEL prays openly for a quick death."

## VI. Dachau XI: Bauunternehmung L. Moll (p. 318–19)

"Noon. The thermometer's red needle falls to −15
Celsius. The *Kapo* orders us to the kitchen for tea.
A liquid—grassy, but hot. ISRAEL sits on a stump,

holding a thin metal cup in long, skeletal hands.
He swallows slowly, warming his fingertips,
and turns to me saying something, something

I must ask him to repeat. He emits another
raspy sound and falls. The interest his death
arouses in those near us is in his clothes.

But we chase the scavengers away. MAKS
and I lift ISRAEL, a man neither brother
nor relative, yet both and more, and carry him

to the woods, a safe distance from the latrines.
Just then an SS urinating behind a frozen bush
leaps out and with his rifle he insists we bury

our friend in the snowy hole for excrement.
Silently, without making trouble, as ISRAEL
would have wished, we go back to the camp."

# The Last Blue Light

If this is my last flight may I still
have time to taste the darkness

melting on my tongue, dissolving
with the sound of sugar maple leaves

blowing around my childhood home;
may wind lift the leaves up to their branches

and air be restored to the last season,
winter's steamy breath leaving us autumn,

all shovels and rakes remaining in dust.
Unneeded. Let us reach our altitude,

each of us humming our assent, moving
with the sounds of wet machinery. Nothing

visible as we bear down through space
but the last blue light of day, glowing

at the black wings, the seat belt sign now off
and my dead friend, Michael, sleeping

in the empty row beside me. The fire highlights
in his poker-straight ponytail lighting up the aria

on his lap, the one he dozed off memorizing,
the day his plane went down,

his thick lips still shivering and blue
from the icy waters off La Guardia.

*Nothing yet has edged us out of the sky,*
he says, to show he's listening. Each of us now

weighs as much as the city we grew up in.
And I can almost feel this sense

of being occupied, of the stampede
of population—

everyone I've ever loved
moving through rows of starlight,

and in me,
and what if the dead need us, too,

as much as we need them?
And who wouldn't give

everything if it meant
having them among us, alive again?

# Lament for My Brother

Many nights these days he's out beneath the stars,
a bottle of single malt in a brown bag
that wrinkles in his hand like a shrunken head,
walking with his friend, Ken, and a girl from work,
all from night shift. Tonight they've all worked
doubles, they're wired, the air electric in their lungs.
Ross takes a swig, wipes the lip with his sleeve,
and hands the bottle off to light a cigarette,
exhaling the storm cloud upward into night.
He thinks he sees his whole future in the smoke.
*What'll you have?* he says to smoky figures,
wiping out the inside of a rinsed-off shot glass.

Ken jangles the keys and says, *My place.*
The three walk in. They light a joint
and lie back on the bed, still gazing at stars.
My brother nestles his thigh against the girl's.
All three pass the limp ashen knuckle
from their fingers to their lips. O night!
tonight spare them the day's demands,
let them be unaware of death, that other
sleep, and grant them every wish. Let them
breathe in the crisp night air you were perhaps
saving for autumn, and let them be here forever,
where lakes have thawed and walleye swim again.

# The Insomnia Room

The image that possesses you and never leaves your side in anguish
and insomnia keeps you alive.

                              Guillaume Apollinaire

## *I.*

Lately when I see you it is in darkness
        crouched on a sofa, holding a cigarette
but not taking that slow-drag yet,
blue ribbons of smoke unspooling up your arms,
        a general's epaulets,
the white hair wreathed in blueness
swirling a momentary crown
        for this small but vital nation of one

among the porch-lit kingdoms
        of the sleepless; the feathered headdress
of smoke vanishes above you
out the screened-in window to the right
        where white crests of starlight
break on a black shore; you take
the hit, breathe in every bit of what I see
        comically first as an exploding straw

but come to love regarding as a torch.
        Then a handheld sparkler, then
the smallest flag I've ever seen
for any nation-state, the only banner I know
        set fire to by its king.
The red embers
underline your gestures,
        a lassoed shooting star

in the small cosmos you are keeper of, custodian to.
        You cradle the ashes
of spent smokes, three long gray child
mummy fingers crumbling
        in your free hand, and you keep doing
this trick with your false tooth, making it fall away
& reappear inside a pumpkin grin. This strange night
        of dogs howling in the distance

and me bed-headed, in footed animal pajamas
        afraid that the apple seeds
I've eaten will take root in my stomach.
I walk to the back of the house toward the lake,
        drowning this thought out to the sound
of waves, and find your face,
the face of Auden in old age, a mask of worry
        and melted wax, but made to look

entirely of tears
        hardened to salty glacial faults, strata,
the head epicenter to a brewing
human weather system. You try to rub the lines
        of worry from your face
with air and smoke. But weariness is now
so much a part of you. You drop a cold
        solution in each red eye, the answer to

your incapacity:
        your eyes are no longer able to
make tears. I sit with you a long time
unspeaking in the darkness.
        The tears now come easily.
You smile, head tipped back to distant
music.
        When your false tooth disappears.

*II.*

Tonight alone in another house I look for you having dreamt that
I am

dead again and can't find anyone I've loved. So I start turning this
image

of you inside me sideways, peeling at its emulsion, to see what's
inside:

The '28 Packard on display in Dearborn at Henry Ford's Museum
which you rebuilt

from scratch and scraps over weekends spread across three years,
blue arc-light

turned now shining through keyholes, beneath the converted
garage, its

dark-chocolate-colored door. Blue light reaching outside a study
weaved in starlight

and outer space chirps and tweets. The ham radio's red needle
quivering

Cold War conversations in radio waves that reached voices behind
the Iron Curtain:

The unrecorded static chat. Photos of Harry & Elmer, your brothers.
Two men

destroyed by the Great War who lived. You said, "The freedom to change your

life comes with a price." I want to find what you took to the grave, what's hidden,

say, in your billfold, the image of Mary, your mother, dying in Ohio of weariness

masquerading as heatstroke brought on by midsummer, on a child's birthday.

The shot of Mary carrying the cake she made the child, the one of Mary

falling, and the cake. And my favorite, the one of Mary at someone's door, handing

the cake to someone, probably a parent, now a gray blur, the cake's white helmet

of icing and its maker overcome in sunlight. Mary's hand-off her last voluntary

act before she fell away. I want what Mary tossed across the Baltic Sea, in Poland

and Lithuania, with her Jewish past, keeping this history from everyone. Or if

anyone did know, nobody spoke of it. (Not even you!) I almost never learned. All

eight of you, Mary's children, now are gone. I want to show you this picture

of your sister, Vesta, the last to fall away. The view of her telling Mary's
secret

on a porch between servings of yellow potato salad and sliced canned
pears floating

like pink walruses in red Jell-O. This close-up of her leaning forward,
looking

like you, and so like Auden. But an Auden sweating in a '50s summer
dress, pink

sandals, pearl earrings, blue wig; the white crumpled handkerchief
resembling

the folded notes you once carried to her for your best friend over miles
in trouser

pockets, overalls, sweated on love letters: TO VESTA FROM EUGENE.
They would

be married for fifty some odd years. It's different for me I am alone at
the end

of love and I want you to stay up with me again one last time. At this
hotel.

On the edge of this continent, by a nightmarish sea that hisses tonight
through the

wisteria. Bring what you will to me, what you once gave, say, at a backyard
casino

gambling to earn money for a church. You played numbers you had no
stake in

and didn't believe and you kept winning anyway. You said, "Remember,
we are

trying to give what we have away." And I got up on tiptoes and emptied
my pockets

on a number, and your hand came down on mine, and I held on, and I lost
everything.

# Song for an Empty Hand

This is my bit of bottled moonlight, my lightning bolt.
This, my What-have-you-done-for-me-lately?
my place where men are separated from the boys
and then reintroduced, more susceptible to beauty

and to love. In the long night of the body, the mind
climbs out of its snail-shell ear. Like an owl.
Its head turns, impossibly around, before it flies
over whole continents of feeling. Snow squalls

raging in the rust belt do not deter it, nor do
the Himalayas, the Mojave, or Beijing;
skinheads in Vienna, the bones of Mogadishu.
May even the horrors of the earth lengthen its wings.

And the body is beautifully there, like hoarfrost.
Tears on its face now glimmering like dimes
falling from a slot machine, or a stream, thought lost,
that breaks through fresh snow at wintertime.

# Yom HaShoah in Florida

In remembrance of the Holocaust, observed in the Hebrew calendar
on the anniversary of the Warsaw Ghetto Uprising

Here, the trees pay their respects, mourn openly,
      wear dreadlocks of hanging Spanish moss
sun bleached ash-blue and swaying; in seawind
      they become prayer shawls
salted with dust, grief threads of every kind
      of human hair, some washed ashore
in mollusk shells, some rescued from mass graves,
      appearing now as storm-torn curtains,
silver-blue and smoke-stained, as tattered
      boas flapper-thrown from bygone

Mardi Gras, sweat-ruined scarves and handkerchiefs
      hanging like empty hives of dried lilac
& wisteria. Squinting and sweaty in the midday heat
      I can almost believe they shine for the
unlikely blessing on Tadzik, my Ohio pediatrician,
      who emerged from a Warsaw Ghetto
bomb-flooded cellar & walked out drenched
      into the clutches of laughing armed SS
and lived. The Gestapo, in laughing, forgot
      to shoot Tadzik and the nurses—Bela,

Sabinka—his fiancée Fredzia, her brother, Henio.
      Maybe if I stare long enough I will see that
these trees wear the torn clothes of the vanquished
      like medals: Bela's torn blouse, her
skirt and underthings ruined at Umschlagplatz
      by Gestapo who pulled her by those prized
blonde streaming curls into another room . . .
      . . . and, later, on the train ride

to Treblinka, when Bela kissed Fredzia & said
      "Help me" and her hostaged

friends lifted her up together, up, like a child,
      up to the window without glass
—the train's pistons pumping furiously now—
      her wish to fly finally fulfilled
when she pushed herself from the cattle car,
      as Pinek had instructed her,
and how in leaping she became a paper moth,
      before the rush of bullets pinned her
to the sky above the sun-scorched earth;
      if I look hard enough, I will see

these heaps of Spanish moss are the spun
      legacy of Henio Grin, the strewn yarn
of his lost story, for which there are still
      not words enough. Not for Henio,
who was sixteen and would not live to see
      another time. He was the first one
off the train at Majdanek, winning the prisoners'
      race easily—by two whole lengths—
to the gated building beyond a field of dust,
      turning around an instant to cheer on

his slower friends, certain his track-star speed
      would save him, though it would not.
Only Tadzik, who stumbled, was saved
      when the SS egging them on held out
a white-gloved hand to block Tadzik's last-place
      finish to the death showers, an act both
merciful and arbitrary. My doctor was shoved
      aside, and the Gestapo said: "You
idiot" and "Don't be afraid, your death won't
      amount to one flash of lightning

in the night sky." And what if the trees in Florida,
           covered as they are with Hawaiian
leis and luau dancers' skirts & struck piñatas
           whose treasures kids made off with
long ago, are also a kind of code still waiting
           to be cracked, saved tickertape & streamers,
fanfare for homecoming parades that won't happen
           till everyone comes home. Or they are
the nests of promises, each strand thrown
           by a spouse whose marriage vows

extend beyond the grave; the mosses certainly are
           woven of Bela's braids, and countless others,
which now smell forever of summer & brush
           fires near everglades. For each specter circling
the earth, and all who still believe blue Shoah smoke
           shall block *our* way to Paradise, the trees
observe this breach, the break in covenant. Listen.
           How gently they rattle their worry beads
for us on a day that begins in Hebrew at sunset.
           When the first three night stars are visible.

II

# Preparing for Flight

All I need is this phonebook, this tasty freeze, this . . .

Steve Martin, *The Jerk*

All I need is this square of sunlight falling through me,
the runway out there, bending out of sight. All I need
is the scar above my lip to speak. The antechamber

to flight is filled with cell phones and neon highlighters,
pink, green, violet and every color in between. People
play with their thumbs and bottom lips and double-chins.

The man across from me talks inventories and bottom
feeders, and signing off, and moving forward, and what's up?
And that's just tossing $23,000 into the garbage! that's

just a heads-up, he says. I want that language to find itself
lost and returned to splendor. I want it to pull down its pants
and stick out its shiny ink-black tongue. I want it to be afraid.

I want that man to listen to the woman with the lump in
her throat, she's talking suicide at cheetah speed. It seems her
would-be husband got cold feet. I want him to find a way inside,

to go to her, like the friend who holds her now, and let her
know that she is better off. Just so we are on the same page,
the suit beside him says. Just so we understand each other,

love. I was just checking the numbers. I just put out a voice
mail. I'm trying to crunch the figures, love, to fax them to you
via ESP. But now it seems the light's flipped on its side,

angling like a salmon. Or a prism. I want to resist all talk
of bottom-lines. Maybe I'll fax this to you, maybe I won't,
but sure as starlight and this man's fierce business-sense,

the dream-life of everything we love and lay our hands upon,
we're on the edge of something luminous. I know we are. So often
now, dear one, I thought my back would break before it,

before this scrub-jet would arrive, and I could get to you.

# Flashlight Stories

*1.*

The women in this family play pinochle,
smoke, toss back salted nuts with the dregs
of their drinks. Ethel, Gladys, Esther,

Vesta, Effie—names you can't imagine
anyone being named again. One would say,
Richard, would you like more to eat?

The men are out back still taking turns
grinding the ice-cream maker, their biceps
swollen and warm from crushing the ice

to slush. One by one, even the laughter
of these ghosts becomes less audible.
You want to ask them in, to tell them stories

by flashlight to make them want to stay.
You could begin with anything, anything—
the smallest thing that ever made you want your life.

2.

The air after rain. The sounds of lovers
making love, tea and toast, and nevertheless
going about their days. It has something

to do with gravity. One moment you're walking
at the edge of a street, when your brother
is taken from your hand. You go your whole life

thinking, Why him and not *me?* You wake
and are no longer young. Traffic is still insidious,
but now the hours come apart like soft-boiled eggs.

You spoon the round bellies out, pour on tabasco,
grind fresh pepper, eating the moments so they
sizzle in your mouth, so they burn as they go down.

It takes a kind of courage, sometimes, just to say it.
Whole days spent otherwise have proven this to me.
Step forward, and the wind braces you on all sides.

## 3. *Ghost Story*

In the tent, we point the flashlights toward the roofs
of our mouths and flick the switch. Like wax heads
from *Grauman's Chinese Theatre* my best friends become
two terrifying African death masks. We shiver; the rain
falls harder through the maples and our friend tells us
how his father tore open his knees running home from school,
went swimming anyway, and heard eerie muffled voices
coming from the docks; how he moved toward them,
and they pulled him from the water, pointing at a spot
now teeming with shark fins. I pull the scratchy blanket
around my neck, and another says that his great-grandmother's body
was kept uncovered in his mother's childhood living room for days
before her funeral; and one night his mother watched through tears
as her bedroom door dissolved, her grandmother walked in
and kissed her, once, on the temple, the way she always did.

*4. Fender Strat with Wah-Wah, Fuzz Box, & Whammy Bar*

A smeared note swells and scatters
like a voice inside a cave, tugging
the vibrato till the sound divides

like an egg yolk dropped in broth;
inside you now, swirling like a geyser
trapped in earth before the whole thing

blows apart. As if the spirit-world will
talk back, the more you face the amp
and lean into yourself. You think,

there are so many ways to pray. This being,
of course, another lining up of hands,
the way to take the vagrant silence in yourself

and make it deafening. Now it is the whole house
breaking in the sound of surf, the echoes
rattling the bookshelves, even without the sound.

## 5. *One Underworld*

My seventeenth summer, sweating all day
long in the underbelly of a local Y, breathing in

a boiler room's dry furnace heat.
The sun-scorched janitor tells me

how the whores in Vietnam
unclasped their necklaces and moved them

bead by bead

inside you; and when you came
pulled out that headless rattlesnake so fast

your entire body would explode.
And something then would silver

in your mind, and napalm would spill
its orange acid from the trees. And everything,

for that one moment, would be still
and perfect and impossible to bear.

## 6. My Mother's Bed on Fire

First there were just a few zeros
singed perfectly like nihilist monograms
in her elegant nightclothes. Full moons
blackened at their edge. A nightstand;
the ashtray by her bed overflowing

with a pile of broken doll fingers
with lipstick at the ends where
the life-force had been sucked away.
When it finally happened, we were lucky:
She woke up.

And the insurance covered everything.
Now it's the best room in the house.
We joke about it now; call it her Pleasure Dome.
When I talk about visiting, she says: Bring
your girlfriend, honey, and you can sleep in it.

## 7. *Taking a Shower with My Father*

After I dislocated my shoulder the second time
I stood in the shower of a local Y with my father,
onion-bellied men lathering themselves, lemon
meringue froth running off their bodies, inching
across the tile and down the drain.

When he saw me unable to wash myself,
he spread a cloud of soap across my back.
He said, The guys are going to think
we're queer, ha! Let them! And I'm the one
getting nervous, eyeing the doorway,

calming myself with thoughts of the house
he had in Michigan with his second wife.
When I had nightmares there, no matter what,
he'd open the coverlet like a storm-cellar door
in tornado season, still half-asleep, to let me in.

## 8. Arcana Mundi

After the divorce Mom read every book she could
find on the Afterlife, Divination, Atlantis, Lost Worlds.
Ancient Cities. At some holiday party she discovered
a gift for hypnosis, channeling. One by one she held
the willing in waking sleep, walked them backward
through their lives to who they were before they were.
*It came so easily.* We sat in elementary and she taught
Special Ed at a country school in Salem. By day, her kids
basked in the glow of an incubator bought out-of-pocket,
the speckled eggs warming until they hatched. At night
she read Seth Speaks, roamed the darkest rooms inside
herself to find the opening. *When other voices came.* As if
some station buried deep inside our skulls broadcast
a music you could learn to tune in. When the voices
finally came for her, the flood of static never went away

## 9. *The Temple*

Before they even knew what
it could do to you, they pulled back
my mother's lovely midnight hair,
a moon and its reflection rising
at each temple, two strong men
pinned her down, put electrodes there,
a pincher here—cold metal on teeth
on tongue—and fired up the furnace

to her brain. the shock, electricity,

shrugging through her body, oh, oh,
she told me she heard the woman in the bed
beside her moan, as if on fire, already bending
at the knees. She still hears the woman screaming
sometimes at night, the screaming wakes her
and she says, herself, "My God, it's me!"

*10. Alarm*

By your thirtieth year they say
*it* should manifest. If not, in most cases,
you have been spared.

But there *are* exceptions.

Even two years beyond my third decade
the dormant, snaky coil of DNA
       might hiss itself

awake, snap its distorted spine
and strike. But my mother says: "Honey
       as long as you can point to
a reason you feel a certain way

you don't have what I have." And even now
I am afraid I feel the alarm about to go off in me,
       the harried beating in my neck's

carotid artery, the green branching veins

inside my wrists. See now, if you can't feel it here,

the second hand ticking its true course,

a heart pre-set to detonate.

*II.*

Sometimes you have nothing left to say, and still
you keep on muttering like a set of wind-up teeth.
Other days, your eyes just glide across the words.
Like a catamaran. What is it that makes this
the moment you rise into yourself, a set of overalls

that ripple into being? You watch your love hug
what seems to be a beaten horse, just like Raskolnikov.
But when you look later, she wants to console a tree?
She can be so dramatic! Even the old Russian men playing dominoes
in Golden Gate Park look on and scratch their heads.

It's just another fish wrapped in aluminum, they seem to say.
Someone grown heavy with the world, not ready yet to speak.
When my mother woke up from her coma,
the first words to escape her were, I'm hungry!
What if each moment opened up for you like this?

12.

After so much build-up, who should
arrive but the little Thai delivery man
with the white walrus mustache, the one

you always overtip because he is so old
and still delivering dumplings, chicken with lemon grass
on a rainy Friday night. The strangers

you've opened your doors to!
How many times have you held off sleep
just to think again of an idling car

where you could fall in love.
Or the jukebox in your favorite bar,
how it shoots sparkling pink and green

soda pop through its veins. You can never fill
yourself enough with your beloved, you think,
and it seems almost impossible to die.

# III

# All Souls' Eve

Polish Military Cemetery, Kraków

Dusk and so many flowers, lit votives, mourners
who come leaning leggy baguettes on headstones

with vodka shots, steaming containers of soup—

some open their gifts directly on the graves.
One woman, a friend, upends the local pilsner,

her dead man's pleasure, and the piss-steam

hisses a hillside specter. I'm here but somewhere
else: my mind, racing, moves at the speed of dreams.

The woman's son climbs from my shoulders

and sprints the length of cobbled graveyard wall
toward some inscrutable fury, becoming all voice

—like the white-bearded cantor on Rosh Hashanah

who for one vast moment arrived at a resonance
I could almost taste

as it held us alive and at the brink of shattering.

You pay a price for this—for all this nosiness.
In rooms where you are not wanted, a light
goes out. Venetian blinds blink once and close.
The heat that comforts you speckles your sight.
That dread-locked man with the white cane knows:
*You pay a price.* He told me he knows the night
we know, but all the time. Sometimes it glows
around the edges like a blind made bright
from behind.
                   But often it does not.
He sleeps, and the darkness darkens more.
It covers his face like strands of lover's hair.
He takes them in his hands, rubs the cornstalk
silk and scent across his skin. The paramour
unlocks the room now opening on air.

## Insleave for *A Hieroglyphic Key to Spiritual Mysteries:*
## Published Posthumously in Stockholm, 1784

*for Emanuel Swedenborg*

What *cannot* be said of a scientist
who blamed his toothaches on demons,
lost his teeth as an old man
and grew others? When he discovered

there was no Hebrew word for ecstasy
he grew a labyrinth in his garden.
And when he found it lacking
he built a pyramid of glass

and opened all its mirrored doors.
Once he turned a prism for hours
until it made a view of a garden
and its inner door. Then he turned it

inward, focusing on the blood as nexus
for the soul. The gardeners saw him
calling out to nothing, mouthing words
to shadows and vacant chairs.

Then they remembered the prophet
Ezra, how he heard the voice
and drank from the floating cup,
growing wise and drunk on what-

ever passed through him. They knew
visions were more than *tardemah*,
more than madness of deep sleep,
for when he woke, he remembered

everything. Like him, their master
woke prepared to advise them in matters
of the soul, to explain correspondences
between invisible worlds and words,

but held his tongue, having reached
into the foggy entrance of silence,
the horizon uniting the seven waters
and sky, to be lifted, carried far

and returned, if only to bring back
the dense colors rising there, scarlet
spreading over his eyes like a field
of flowers in the distance, blossoming.

# The Four-Legged Man

*1.*

I was conceived in an ordinary bed
inside the family house, my uncle Lester
listening, perhaps finding himself
beneath the new box springs. I heard

my mother's mother was a witch,
or so father said. At any rate, she liked
to make them tea, the brew steeped
in a vat that glimmered whale-blood orange—

that settled in them uneasily, stained
their mouths cornflower blue. The same tea
the doctor sipped before he had me breathe,
and found another heart that hammered

in a sunken hull of bone. I've never been
alone. I am *all* Gemini. Among the Hall
of Curiosities, we're home. The swallower
of snakes shared us lodgings for a season

and I paid him back tenfold when his constrictor
vanished in its cage. I heard the blind-girl scream,
the ringmaster's only daughter, on whom
it set to strangling, undid the yard-long thigh of it,

wiped snake-spit from her face, pampered
her, and still performed. That night, I found
the twin rope walkers, red costumes pulled soundlessly
in silhouette and spilled about our lamp.

2.

Word got around of our proclivities.
The dwarves, the barker's girls, the loveliest—
the fallacies of how we freaks make love
were put to bed. I have four normal daughters,

twins, with former acrobats; three sons
fathered by my brother's legs. They visit
when we're in town. At carnival, our city
blinks like fireflies, and no one eyes us twice.

Throughout, the children see things strange
or stranger than their dads: muskmelons
from Ottawa shaped like a sheriff's mistress
coupling with a squid.
                                        Sights to make Jesus
weep—the pickled two-headed fetus, a hell
of mirrors, with other horrors under glass.

3.

The grinder says a freak is either born
or made. But he is paid to lie. The congress
I have known is complicated: that pickled
fetus with two heads is something else,
a blown anomaly; a shrug perfected.
Life murdered by the marvel that it made.
Among the sideshow's armory, I've seen

the wonders taken from tribal villages:
Nairobi kings, their queens, and pygmies
shackled in their sleep. I've wakened to their cries:
uncomprehended squalls that weathercock
their points; nightmares of ordinary men,
made palpable in ear-locked cells. I need
these other lives to speak about myself.

Do you know the story of the royal Yoruba
who made himself the Mudfish King?—he was
about to give a speech and could not move.
He slapped his cold, hard legs like lifeless fish,
said "I'm of *both* worlds!" The crowd went wild.
There, cripples are put to death. I've lived the terror
of *that* life, and more, and this.
                                    They say
I will awaken one morning—no feeling below
my neck, feverish with the plot of my last dream:
Therein, I carry a crippled boy like matchwood
from a blackened building, undersides of tongues
and smoke wreathing our heads. Before I make it
out the door, I lose my grip. He falls,
orange-robed, a Buddhist hallowed in flame.

# Visions of Captivity: Neulengbach, 1912

*For Egon Schiele*

## 1. Crude Hours Which Pass Over Me Like Animals

Even now I do not understand
the spat and hissed and murmured words
strangled out of throats in distant cells;
harangue of murderers

and petty thieves washes over me
each night, until it is too wet to sleep,
and I paint these prison walls to dry.
Only later do I fathom

the content of their noise: the story
*Why have I been buried here?*
By morning my chronicle disappears,
pulled into masonry

by some animal of unknown origin.
Dust, webs, bile, sediment
from sweat and soot cover the plaster
of this cage. Stains darkest

where my bed touches the wall and white-
washed lime rubs off and comes unsheathed.
*It's frightening. Now, even a fire*
*In my cell would be*

*beautiful.* Tomorrow, the guard
will let my friend bring watercolors.
Thoughts diffuse after dusk. I hear
Trieste, the sea, and open in.

## 2. *The Room In Which An Orange Is The Only Light*

I paint the cot in my cell,
the corridor, and rubbish of inmates.
Draw the organic movement

of the water-pour, the unsightly chair.
Smudging color to give them shape.
Last night: hoarfrost; the trembling.

Moans—distant, soft; desperate.
At last the minor angels of apathy
stretched out their numb and fragile limbs

upon the frightened dying, dressing them
in sleep. The eye of every other god
now far from here or gazing elsewhere.

Not even their dander falls to us.
Herewith the stink of sweat and lye,
the rot of wool and linen, an orange.

V. brought it yesterday. Last night, it was
my only light, that small *indefatigable*.
*It did me unspeakable good.*

## 3. The Trial: Lord, Open Your Jeweled Eyes

The irretrievable hours have sifted.
A courtroom near Vienna. A gavel
slams. Order. Uncharged and held
without bail, here I learn my crime:

Impropriety. That young vagrant
haunts me still. She came to my room
one night, disrobed, insisting she work
for rent; and though underage, unlovely,

I obliged. Now the judge intrudes
my designs, manhandles the parchment
of her, the study confiscated when
they pulled me from my bed. Lifted

to his lamp, he thumbs the parted legs,
the darker creases of her sex, where it
did not reach light. He adjusts the wick,
beholds her from within. *Pornography.*

This unfinished nude, not my best,
unnerves me. I could show them things—
they would bury me alive. Above,
the paper seal glows amber over

flames and air looms, fragrant. I've
known whores whose hair smelled like
this, burning in bedside lamps.
What the judge does now is willful,

sleight of hand. The darkening parchment
gains circumference like a black hole
he threads the fire through. The moon
enlarges rapidly—a monk's hairline

instantly receding at the crown, taking
in its flame, her skin. Embers sprawl
to the bailiff's box, wind scattering
her crushed bones like mice in white scrawl.

IV

# Poem Buried in a Line by Paul Éluard

*I stand before this landscape* at dusk
    jacklighted, caught in the highbeams,
shocked into stillness, rapt, incapable
    of flight before the evening's radiance.
I stand in front of everything I've done
    knowing what happens if I don't move—
a horn blows, and I run across the street.

    In front of everyone I have ever loved
and lied to, I stand, the scorpion I am,
    pinned to my shadow, on display,
like an insect still pleading in its case
    of amber, in a collection of private griefs
hereby assembled, dusted and labeled
    by specialists who isolate each flaw

beneath a beam. I stand before the last
    red light of day that rages like the bloodbaths
that stain my country, noise of a distant train
    and my shrunken heart still fluttering
in its bone-case. In front of my mother
    and her cracked ribs, I stand after
the accident, when she was unable to sleep

    except in chairs, living from pill to pill,
and the distance between my father and me
    quickening, after his illness, each day
a few more words dissolving from
    his tongue and lips; or sprouting wings
like the long-legged mayflies that keep
    heaving their bodies against my windows

at night, desperate to get in and fling
    themselves at anything luminous.
Sometimes I catch one before it smolders;
    I open the door with one hand cupped
and set it free. I stand before you now,
    my future, love, and all the lost words
keep flapping their nervous wings

    like the only bird that ever flew
into my hands; it pecked my cuticles,
    pecked my watchband long enough
for my brother to drive home to wake
    our sister, so she could stand there
and see what had flown down to us:
    a balled-up love letter, breathing,

impossible to believe. I stand again
    on a gray-toothed coast, stacking stones
till they are columns the sky leans on.
    The ocean spits up more pieces to its stories;
some we pocket, throw back or bury,
    each a part of something beyond itself,
like us, unfathomable, *like a branch on fire*.

# Artisans of the Tomb

They love their utensils: the perfume
bottles shaped like Nile fish, the bowels
of sky binding Helios in lotus flowers, spoons
carved as bound oxen. In treebark, blown
sand, any surface falling into shape
they discern profiles of angels, faces
lost to famine, plague. I watch the scribe
Nebmerutef palm the blank scroll.

He prays for words and waits hours
to touch bone, the spine rising
in darkness. A constellation of thorns
catching fingers, eyes, figures emerge
like veins to sculptor's hands, tracking
the pulse of stone, the rock inlaid with breath.

# Figure Painting at the School of Fallen Angels

One day these cloven youths shifting weight
behind dark canvases will paint the fall of man—
even the least promising, fashioned in black,
will be filled by a higher motive grinding colors,
mixing the spirits that thicken his medium;
the others hover a nude like flies on a lake.
Amanda, the suicide, whose perfect breasts
are wasted here on the shades, backlit by
the damned, will lie down in the mind that paints
an afterlife for her, rendering the boiling waters
obsolete; and Gia, the blue-lipped diva
of thrift-store veneer, will throw her oil brush
to have a final smoke; and all the patient masters here—
Leonardo, Paul Gauguin, Van Gogh, that reddened
palette knife, demanding nothing but everything
from the most able artisans who even now
pour over the endless inlays of anatomy
that each day grow more and more unneeded.

*Moravia, 1801*

The fever kept him working, waking—writing
held off the other realm, even as it distilled
a room made fragrant by larkspur and woodsmoke.
He stoked the fire, ink plumed in his moving—

the heat from him warmed the night he wanted
to expose. At twenty-five, he nearly did, died
ploughing the hours. He watched them burn
in daybreak's furnace. Not enough, he had to learn

the afterlife. His first Virgil was a dream,
*it dreamed* to *him*—he died and came back
to life climbing a rocky gorge, scree crumbling
at his feet. He tumbled down a shaft

and found an unmined passageway. Steam
hissed off the walls. Sparks on alluvium
and groundwater played about the cavern
and his feet. The light hove cold and blue,

and higher cliffs arose with brighter veins. There
he saw it, the blue flower, though it altered
as he approached to pluck it. The corolla dissolved.
His coughing woke him, wrecked him (or his father's

hammer did) and broke the spell like molten iron
that flares red till it is beaten sideburn white,
*yearning* melted to a silver ounce of meteor,
star-chipped light, now fallen through a crater

in the firmament. Like crystals formed
where lightning strikes, translations of the sky.
Inverted celestial. What might have flowered
from Novalis and his apprenticeship mining

the darkness, snaps synapse, flashes out of vision.
Consumption darkened his Eurydice, ink-line
broken, (he wrote) *We are the midpoint of emanations—*
the certain flourish of a stallion now hemmed in.

# A Brief Folklore of Typography

An orange turns black
on a column
to make the letter i.

A servant lights a match,
holds it to a burner on a god's stove
and turns the dial. To give fire
more of its element
makes an exclamation.

The twig that holds the apple
coils into a serpent.
The first question appears
before the eyes.

A Salem woman set free
from the stockade;
or sperm moments before
reaching the egg.
Each makes ";" a totem
to momentary finality.
The sign something is coming
and the end is near.

A remote star
blackens by spraypaint
above the arthritic
finger in the i.

And the ellipses following
like mouths of children
waiting to find out
how the story ends.

# A Visionary's Company

Fact is I *was* illiterate & sign'd
      our wedding papers with an X.
But my Brilliant William knew, more than
Myself, the treasure lurking there,
      beneath the batter'd fallen cross
Of anonymity. He felt
    an affinity

For my straining hand, & taught me to use
      a brush, a pen. In Time, I learn'd
Meter, too. I lov'd to make up nonce verses
To Songs I sang to cheer him as I rubb'd
      his back & neck. It's true:
Often my William was
    in Paradise.

But when he return'd, he brought back
      all those images to me. I always believ'd
His Work would live beyond us, & really
Could not say, How or Why
      or When—but often I dreamt the Angels of
Transport were tapping out new Songs in our room:
    *Catherine Blake!*

I'd hear, & come around to see him
      caught within another dream, his small hand
Moving to thoughts it never held
Before. My mind would empty a moment
      all that it knew; our house in Lambeth
Would expand, & I'd feel short of breath, near faint.
    My eyes beheld

The Spirits ascending from those words,
        clapping their hands in joy, as I
Imagine William was upon their making.
Daily, hourly, he held counsel with Spirits
        & then with me. We were interrupted once,
By his patron—a certain Mr. Butts!—
        while reciting passages from

*Paradise Lost*. In our garden, utterly
        nude, with our ridiculous friend
Stammering apologies, tipping his
Bowler hat repeatedly. Of course,
        we asked him in. What did we care?
*We* were unasham'd. Indeed we were too
        much for him. He fled.

We laughed for quite some Time about it, & then
        My Husband got that look again,
& wanted us to try our hands at prophecy.
He ask'd that I look to the book at hand
        to divine my fortune, Bysshe's *Art of Poetry*,
Upon whose hand-worn cover I wrote a poem
        regarding the joys

Of sensual experience. William was so well pleas'd
        with my fortune, he tried his hand at it.
He lighted on a verse from Dryden's
Virgil. The one that says a tree
        "withstands the wrath of the elements"
Due to its "fixed foundations."
        He liked that phrase;

It reminded him of his first vision as a child;
        walking the London countryside,
He saw among the ditches & blacken'd kilns
A tree swarming with Angels, & all kinds of

lumina specking the boughs
Like stars. He ran home to tell his father
        who nearly beat him for lying;

Will said: "A fool does not see the same tree
        a wise man sees." Regrettably, it was
No easier for me. He always boasted of what he call'd
*Our* visitations. I should have had them! He show'd me
        *Where* to look for them! But only since
His Death, when his assistant,
        Mr. Richmond

Kiss'd his cheek, & clos'd His Eyes
        "to keep the visions in" have I enjoy'd
Unearthly company—two & three hours a day
Or more. As though he were still here! Though
        mostly we speak of how best to market
His engravings; only seldom do we revel
        in Eternity.

# Notes

Cover: The cover photo shows Solomon Schechter studying the Cairo Genizah, located in the Ezra Synagogue in Fostat (Old Cairo, Egypt), built in 882. Although several people visited the *genizah* in the 1700s and 1800s, no one formally examined it because of the superstition that claimed disaster would befall anyone who touched the sacred pages. Nevertheless, various pages were occasionally stolen or sold.

In 1896, two Christians brought some leaves to Solomon Schechter, professor of Talmudic and rabbinical literature at Cambridge University. Schechter recognized them as the Hebrew original "Book of Wisdom," ascribed to Ben Sira. The Book of Wisdom became part of the Christian biblical cannon (Ecclesiastics) when translated into Greek. Before its discovery in the Cairo Genizah, no known Hebrew version existed, and some scholars doubted its existence. Schechter led an expedition to Cairo where, over several painstaking months, he extracted thousands of pages and took them back to Cambridge.

More than 200 previously unknown poems by Yehuda Halevy (c. 1080–1145) were found in the *genizah*. Perhaps the most important papers found belong to Rabbi Moses ben Maimon (Maimonides or the "Rambam," 1135–1204), the greatest medieval Jewish philosopher and physician. The *genizah* contained over thirty works authored by the Rambam, including commentary on some Mishna tractates and a number of letters. Before this discovery, only a few lines of original Rambam writings had ever been found.

Today, a large portion of the Cairo Genizah's documents are available at the University Library in Cambridge. Smaller collections are spread out across the world. (These notes rely upon the entry, written by Alden Oreck, in the Jewish Virtual Library, at http://www.jewishvirtuallibrary.org/jsource/History/Genizah.html.)

*"Amchu"*: The photographs described herein may be found in *Warszawskie Getto: 1943–1988 W 45 Rocznice Powstania, Wydawnictwo Interpress: Warsaw, Poland* (1989). Though most of the photos are unattributed, having been discovered well after World War II, the images in the poem were taken in the first months of the Warsaw ghetto by Dr. Tadeusz (Tadzik) Stabholz (née 1916) while he was imprisoned there. These images, and others in the above volume, were smuggled to safety in much the manner that the poem describes.

"Brother Salvage: a *genizah*": The final poem written for this collection is woven from many conversations and details gleaned from Dr. Stabholz's only memoir, *Seven Hells* (Holocaust Library Press, 1990), all of which are gathered here with Dr. Stabholz's encouraging consent. These poems are for him, with my abiding gratitude and love.

Existing factual information on the Israel in the poem is as follows: Israel Sawczyc (listed Sarvezyc at Dachau); born 20 October 1906 in Bialystok, Poland; brought to Dachau from Sachsenhausen (with Dr. Stabholz) on 17 November 1944; died on 23 March 1945; prisoner number #127154.

"Insleave for *A Hieroglyphic Key to Spiritual Mysteries,* Published Posthumously in Stockholm, 1784": Wilson Van Dusen's *The Presence of Other Worlds* (Harper & Row, 1975) and James John Garth Wilkinson's *Emanuel Swedenborg: A Biography* (London: West Newberry, 1849) were extremely helpful, as was Abraham Heschel's *The Prophets* (Jewish Publication Society of America, 1962).

"Visions of Captivity: Neulengbach, 1912": The italicized portions have been revised freely or are quoted directly from the translations in Alessandra Comini's *Schiele in Prison* (New York Graphic Society, 1973).

"Poem Buried in a Line by Paul Éluard": The full line in French, "Je suis devant ce paysage féminin comme une branche dans le feu," (literally: "I am before this feminine landscape like a branch in the fire") is the first and last line to the poem, "Extase."

"Figure Painting at the School of Fallen Angels": This poem is a send-up of Wallace Stevens's "Piano Practice at the Academy of Holy Angels" from *Opus Posthumous* (Knopf, 1957).

"Novalis": The German romantic poet and visionary philosopher, Friedrich von Hardenberg (1772–1801), took his pen name from the Latin word meaning "freshly ploughed fields." Much of the poem was inspired by details from his life and his unfinished novel concerning the development of a poet, *Heinrich von Ofterdingen* (Waveland Press, 1964).

"A Visionary's Company": Peter Ackroyd's *Blake: A Biography* (Knopf, 1995) was indispensable to the writing of this poem.

# Acknowledgments

I want to thank the editors who first published these poems, sometimes in earlier versions, in the following journals:

*Columbia: A Magazine of Poetry & Prose* ("A Brief Folklore of Typography"); *Cream City Review* ("Artisans of the Tomb"); *Michigan Quarterly Review* ("Yom HaShoah in Florida"); *Missouri Review* ("Flashlight Stories": 1–7, 9–12); *Nation* ("The Dangerous Light," "Song for an Empty Hand"); *Paris Review* ("The Four-Legged Man," "Novalis," "Poem Buried in a Line by Paul Éluard," "Visions of Captivity: Neulengbach, 1912"); *Ploughshares*: ("Antique Shop Window, Kraków"); *Poetry* ("A Visionary's Company"); *Salmagundi* ("Insleave for *A Hieroglyphic Key to Spiritual Mysteries,* Published Posthumously in Stockholm, 1784"); *Western Humanities Review* ("Figure Painting at the School of Fallen Angels," "The Last Blue Light," "Preparing for Flight"); *Witness* ("The Insomnia Room").

Poems in the first half of this manuscript appeared in the limited-edition collection, *Preparing for Flight and other poems*, published by Pudding House Press.

Poems from the second half of this manuscript appeared in the limited-edition collection, *A Visionary's Company & other poems,* published by Parallel Press.

"Flashlight Stories" was awarded the Editors' Prize from the *Missouri Review* and was nominated for a Pushcart Prize.

"Lament for My Brother" appears in *I Have My Own Song for It: Modern Poems of Ohio,* edited by Elton Glaser and William Greenway (2002).

"Yom HaShoah in Florida" was reprinted in *Red, White, & Blues: Poetic Vistas on the Promise of America,* edited by Virgil Suarez and Ryan Van Cleave (2004).

*"Amchu"* and "Yom HaShoah in Florida" appear in *Blood to Remember: American Poets on the Holocaust,* edited by Charles Fishman (2007).

I also want to express my deepest ongoing gratitude to the trustees of the Amy Lowell Poetry Traveling Scholarship; the Wisconsin Institute for Creative Writing at the University of Wisconsin in Madison; the Wallace Stegner Fellowship Program at Stanford University; the Djerassi and Ragdale Foundations; the MacDowell Colony; Krakowski Dom Pizarzy in Kraków, Poland; the Liguria Study Center at Bogliasco, Italy; Brechts Hus of Svendborg, Denmark; and the

Vermont Studio Center for the sustaining gifts of time, support, and refuge. Without the generous help of these most benevolent institutions, and the luminous spirits animating and sustaining them, along with many friends and loved ones and mentors who have tended to me over the years, all teachers, these poems would not exist. And my life would be immeasurably diminished.

One such luminous presence that I must single out for special mention is Nancy Reisman, my partner, and happiness. Abiding thanks.